LEARNING TO WALK
WITH HIM

From Reluctant Missionary to Devoted Disciple

Lessons of Faith, Focus, and the Savior's Love

By: Ken Smith

Let's strive to serve and minister to people because we are primarily motivated by LOVE for God and others!

Source: President Cyril Figuerres, "Love is the Motive," 1993

ISBN: 979-8-9956806-0-4

Manufactured in the United States of America

Disclaimer

This book is a personal memoir and reflects the author's experiences, memories, and perspectives. It is not an official publication of The Church of Jesus Christ of Latter-day Saints. References to doctrine, scripture, and Church teachings are offered in a faith-promoting spirit and should not be taken as official statements of the Church.

Author's Note

Events are described as remembered, and while every effort has been made to be accurate, this book reflects personal experience and understanding. Some names and identifying details have been changed to protect privacy.

Scripture and Quotation Notice

Scripture quotations are from the Holy Bible (King James Version), the Book of Mormon, the Doctrine and Covenants, and the Pearl of Great Price. Quotations from modern Church leaders and other sources are used with attribution. Song lyrics and other copyrighted material are quoted only briefly where permitted or have been paraphrased.

DEDICATION

To every missionary who has wondered if they are doing enough, to the parents who kneel and pray for them, and to Jesus Christ, who calls imperfect people, walks with them, and patiently teaches them how to follow Him.

To my wife, my partner, my safe place to land. You believed in me when I was still figuring out why the Lord prompted me to write this book. None of this exists without you.

To my children, who grew up watching their dad try to become who the Lord needed him to be. I hope this book shows you that obedience, even reluctant obedience, is always worth it.

To President and Sister Figuerres, who met a struggling young missionary exactly where he was, loved him anyway, and showed him what it looks like to walk with the Savior. Thirty years later, you are still teaching me.

And to Elder Mike Smith, who spent three days changing the trajectory of a mission and a life, without ever knowing he was doing it.

MY PRAYER FOR YOU

My prayer for you is that, as you read these pages, you will be guided toward Jesus Christ.

I hope the stories and lessons here point you to Him, not to me, not to numbers, and not to perfection.

If you are preparing to serve, already serving, or quietly wondering if you are doing enough, my prayer is that you will feel God's love for you personally.

I hope you will recognize the Spirit when He speaks to your heart and come to know the Savior not just as a doctrine, but as a living presence in your life.

If anything in this book strengthens you, comforts you, or brings you closer to Him, please know that it did not come from me alone.

My prayer is that this book helps you trust Him more fully and follow Him more faithfully one imperfect step at a time.

PREFACE
ABOUT THE BOOK

Ken Smith possesses a deep and abiding love for young people. He truly desires that you, the readers, will embrace gospel principles that empower you not only as missionaries, but throughout your lives.

This book springs not merely from Ken Smith's study and observations, but from his real-life experiences.

Ken writes with conviction because what he shares has been lived. There is a difference between vicarious learning, learning secondhand through the experiences of others, and experiential learning: learning firsthand through personal revelation and spiritual experience.

A powerful scriptural example of this distinction appears in the account of Nephi. When Nephi first heard his father, Lehi, describe the vision of the tree of life, he understood it secondhand, through vicarious learning. But when Nephi sought and received his own vision, his understanding came through direct revelation by the Holy Spirit, experiential learning. That experience transformed him.

So it was with Elder Smith. What began as vicarious understanding became increasingly experiential. His testimony took root, grew stronger, and has endured now with even greater power over the past thirty-five years.

MY TESTIMONY

I testify that our beloved Heavenly Father and His Son are actively involved in our lives. They direct, orchestrate, and guide us with lovingkindness ("hesed" in Hebrew) with supreme benevolence and exceeding generosity, yet never violating our precious agency.

I am profoundly grateful that they intersected and intertwined Elder Ken Smith's life with my wife's and my own, thirty-five years ago in faraway Kyushu, Japan. I know this was no mere coincidence or random chance. It was a divine design.

That sacred time and place have become, for all of us, one of our personal "waters of Mormon" and "forests of Mormon," a spiritual refuge where we came to know God more deeply and experienced life-changing spiritual transformation.

Paraphrasing Mosiah 18:30, "How beautiful [is Kyushu, Japan] to the eyes of [Elder Smith and President and Sister Figuerres]" because there, they did not merely learn about our Redeemer in a "saber" way, intellectually gaining information and facts about Him. They came to know Him in a "conocer" way: personal, relational, experiential.

Cyril I. A. Figuerres

Mission President, Japan Fukuoka Mission, 1991–1994

TABLE OF CONTENTS

INTRODUCTION

I served a mission for all the wrong reasons.

I didn't go because I had a burning testimony.

I went because I didn't want to break my mother's heart.

I went because all my friends were going, and saying "no" felt impossible.

Maybe that's you. Maybe you went reluctantly, or you're serving right now, wondering whether you measure up.

Maybe you're carrying guilt about not being "spiritual enough," feeling like everyone else has it figured out except you.

Or maybe your story is completely different. Maybe you went with faith and conviction. Maybe you couldn't wait to serve. Maybe your testimony was strong from the beginning.

Either way, these lessons still matter.

Even the most prepared missionary faces moments of doubt, exhaustion, and confusion about what really matters.

Even faithful missionaries wonder if they're making a difference. Even returned missionaries look back and realize there were things they wish they'd understood sooner.

And if you're a parent watching your child struggle halfway around the world, or a leader preparing youth for what's ahead, these lessons may help you support them in ways that truly matter.

What This Book Is & Is Not

This isn't a book of mission tips. It's not a collection of hacks to baptize more people or become a district leader faster.

These are hard-earned truths about what really matters in missionary work, truths that took me far too long to understand.

If you're heading out soon, already in the field, reflecting on your service at home, or supporting someone who's serving, this is for you.

Not because I have all the answers, but because I learned some things the hard way that might help you see your mission, past, present, or future, differently.

These lessons apply whether you're thriving or barely hanging on. Whether you baptize fifty people or none.

Whether you serve for two years, eighteen months, or come home earlier than expected.

Your mission still matters. The Lord measures your offering, not your timeline.

Whether you went prepared or are still trying to figure things out.

Because missionary work isn't about you, it's about learning to represent the Savior. And that's a lesson every missionary, past, present, and future, is still learning.

But first, you need to understand where I started.

Because if God can work with someone like me, He can work with anyone.

A Letter That Became a Book

Years after I returned from my mission, my younger sister left on her own and struggled. My dad asked the family to write her letters of encouragement. I titled mine *"Five Things I Wish I Had Known Before I Served a Mission."*

After I sent it, the letter sat in a drawer for years.

Then I was called to serve as a bishop. When the youth in my ward received their mission calls and began preparing to leave, I updated that letter, printed it, and placed a personalized copy into the hands of each of them before they left. I'm sure I missed someone along the way. If that was you, I'm sorry. Better late than never.

I wanted them to have what I didn't: someone who had been there, telling them the truth about what really mattered.

Over time, as more of them left and returned changed, I felt a quiet prompting that these five lessons needed to reach beyond my ward, one I ignored for far longer than I should have. This book exists because I finally listened.

So here we are.

If God Can Work with Me, He Can Work with You

Those two years in Japan became the most transformative of my life, but they were harder than they needed to be.

Not because missions are supposed to be easy, but because I made avoidable mistakes.

Mistakes that cost me months of unnecessary confusion, frustration, and spiritual pain.

If you went on your mission reluctantly, if you're serving right now and questioning whether you belong there, or if you feel like everyone else has it figured out, I want you to know something:

God doesn't waste anyone's willingness to try.

He took a kid who hated fish and sent him to an island nation where fish is a dietary staple.

He took a kid with no testimony and gave him two years to find one, a harder road than it needed to be. I wouldn't recommend going on a mission without a testimony, not because missions aren't worth it, but because going without one makes everything harder.

He took a kid who went for the wrong reasons and taught him what missionary work is really about.

If He can work with me, He can work with you.

The Five Lessons

Over two years in Japan, as I struggled, grew, and changed, five lessons emerged, five lessons I desperately wish I had known before I left:

1. You never know who you will touch.

2. You are sent where you are sent for a reason.

3. Keep the Savior's life and ministry as the focus in all you do.

4. Don't underestimate the power of prayer and the Lord's love for you.

5. Baptisms aren't the focus; the Savior's love is.

These five lessons are what this book is about. But before we dive into them, you need to understand the rest of my story.

What Comes Next

The Prologue will walk you through my journey from "going through the motions" to actually believing, from opening my mission call in horror to loving Japan and its incredible people more than I ever thought possible.

At the core of every lesson is the same truth: when you make the Savior the center of your mission instead of yourself, your mission becomes what it was meant to be.

Your purpose becomes clearer.

Your struggles become more bearable.

Your joy becomes deeper.

These five lessons reshaped how I understood my mission. But don't just read them, take them to your Heavenly Father. Pray about them. Ask Him what He wants you to learn. Pay attention to what the Spirit teaches you, because what He teaches you personally will be far better than anything I can offer on these pages.

Fair warning: they still won't help you like fish.

PROLOGUE

How I Got Here

Church Without Conviction

I was born to goodly parents who loved the gospel and did everything they could to instill those same values in their seven children. My father followed in his own father's footsteps and joined the Air Force as a pilot.

Every three to five years, the Air Force moved us: Arizona, California, Germany, North Dakota, and Michigan. New homes, new schools, new friends, new wards.

Church was constant. My conviction never was.

Despite growing up in the gospel, I wasn't convinced of its truthfulness, primarily because I didn't try or want to know.

My family expected us to attend church together, so I went through the motions but never developed a real conviction.

Moving had always been exciting until midway through ninth grade, when my father received orders to a base in northeastern Michigan.

A town with one stoplight. A high school in the middle of the woods. And when I asked about their hockey team: "We don't have one." Ouch.

I loved hockey. In North Dakota, it's bigger than football, and I had dreams of playing in college. Now that was gone. Okay, let's be honest, I was a casual hockey player.

In that small Michigan town, I gravitated toward people who struggled with their faith or had none at all. That crowd led me into things not associated with gospel living.

I was just surviving until I could get out and be done with church.

As graduation approached, my father gave me three options for college if I wanted my parents' help: BYU (my grades weren't good enough), Ricks College in eastern Idaho, or Boise State while living with my grandparents (I loved them, but no thanks). Anywhere else, I'd have to pay my own way. I couldn't afford that.

By process of elimination, I was headed to Ricks College. Church-owned, church-run, church everything.

As I packed my car for the 1,800-mile drive to Idaho, my dad gave me a hug and said, "Please go to church."

That tells you everything about my parents' fear that I was leaving the covenant path.

The irony of this move?

Church attendance was mandatory at Ricks. My brilliant plan to escape church involved enrolling at a church-owned school.

When God Showed Up Uninvited

When I checked in at Ensign Hall in Rexburg, I found a yellow sticky note on my welcome packet: "Please call Bishop Allred," along with a phone number.

I thought, *What in the world does he want with me?*

I called less than enthusiastic.

"This is Ken Smith. What do you want?"

I know. I was exuding kindness.

"Well, hello, Brother Smith. I understand you play the piano. I really need someone to play for church tomorrow. Would you be able to do that?"

I had quit lessons at eight, picked the piano back up at twelve, and taught myself all the hymns.

After a long pause and not wanting to embarrass my parents, I reluctantly agreed. A small price to pay to stay under the radar.

The next morning, I sat at a piano in an unfamiliar ward, surrounded by people I didn't know, in a place I didn't want to be.

What happened next caught me completely off guard.

I felt something, something I hadn't felt at other church meetings. Not because it wasn't there before, but because I hadn't wanted it. I hadn't opened myself to it.

That feeling… it was the Spirit of the Lord.

And I kind of liked it.

It didn't hurt that the ward was full of cute girls, an eighteen-year-old's dream.

I decided right then I'd be back the following week.

A few weeks into the semester, several of us were craving Wendy's Frosties. We piled into the back of someone's truck and headed to town.

On the way back, the driver decided to show off his Mario Kart skills. He took a corner way too fast. The truck launched into the air, landed on its side, and skidded down the road.

Remember, we were in the bed of that truck.

I dropped my Frosty and wedged myself between the sides of the truck bed, bracing with my hands and feet to avoid being thrown out.

When we came to a stop, adrenaline pumping, we all walked away, no major injuries.

A miracle.

That night, I had a thought:

If I had died today, I wasn't ready to meet my Maker.

I didn't suddenly become faithful after that experience. But I became aware. And awareness is the first step toward change.

Night after night, I watched my roommate kneel and pray. I worried too much about what others thought of me, and I didn't want him to think I had no faith. So eventually, I started praying too, halfheartedly, defensively.

Heavenly Father… I don't think you're really there… but if you are, give me a sign, and I'll believe.

Wow. Such faith I demonstrated… NOT. If it worked for Laman and Lemuel, maybe it would work for me.

After two weeks of these prayers, something happened.

I came back from class one afternoon and noticed my roommate's Book of Mormon lying open on his desk. From across the room, I could see a single highlighted verse. Part of me said, "Walk away," but another part whispered, "Just look."

After a brief internal battle, curiosity won. I leaned in to read:

Alma 30:44

But Alma said unto him [Korihor]: Thou hast had signs enough; will ye tempt your God? Will ye say, show unto me a sign… all things denote there is a God…

The words pierced me with uncomfortable clarity. That verse might as well have read:

"But Alma said unto KEN: THOU HAST HAD SIGNS ENOUGH!"

My mind flashed to hunting trips with my dad, standing on ridges, watching the sun rise over mountains, the perfect quiet of the plains, how everything fit together.

Korihor was wrong.

So was I.

In that moment, something shifted. The problem wasn't a lack of evidence; it was that I hadn't been willing to see it.

Time passed. All my friends started putting in mission papers. I felt pressured to do the same.

My motivation hadn't changed. I still wasn't serving the Lord; I was just avoiding breaking my mom's heart. So I worked through the process: repented of what needed repenting, confessed what needed confessing, and stopped what needed stopping.

But real repentance, the kind that changes your heart, not just your behavior, I wasn't there yet. That would come later, the hard way.

Eventually, my mission call arrived. I opened it at my friend's apartment. My dad was returning from the first Gulf War that day, so my parents weren't home, and I was NOT going to wait.

I opened the envelope and read:

Fukuoka, Japan.

My friends were excited. I sat in stunned silence.

I HATE fish. Always have. Still do. And God was sending me to an island nation where fish is a dietary staple.

If this was God's idea of a joke, I wasn't laughing.

I stared at the paper, hoping I'd read it wrong. Japan wasn't even on my radar. I didn't know the language, the culture was foreign, and in my mind, it might as well have been the other side of the planet because it was.

My mission started hard.

When we stepped off the plane in Tokyo and heard people speaking, my heart sank. It sounded like they'd taught us the wrong language in the MTC. What I heard around me sounded NOTHING like what we'd practiced.

We had written letters to our girlfriends on the flight and wanted to mail them. We found an information desk and asked, in our best Japanese, for directions to the post office.

My heart sank further when the kind gentleman gave us directions in Japanese, and we couldn't understand a word. He smiled and, in his best English, tried again. We tucked our tails and headed for the post office.

That's when it hit me: I was in over my head.

Two months in the MTC, and I couldn't understand a single sentence.

The first year was brutal.

But the second year became one of the greatest experiences of my life.

I grew to love my mission unlike anything before it.

Before my mission, I dreaded leaving for Japan.

Two years later, I dreaded leaving Japan.

I came to love the culture, the people, the language, everything.

Except the fish. Still can't stand fish.

That transformation happened when I stopped focusing on myself and started focusing on Him, the Savior, and on why He sends missionaries in the first place: not to rack up numbers or impress mission presidents, but to help people feel His love and recognize His Spirit.

Over those two years, five lessons emerged, lessons that answered why I was sent to Japan, and questions I didn't even know I had.

That's what I want for you.

Not perfection.

Not an easy mission.

Not even a lot of baptisms.

I want you to represent the Savior the way He deserves, with your whole heart, not just going through the motions.

The next five chapters dive into those lessons. Some will challenge what you think missionary work is about. Some will feel uncomfortable. Good.

Let's start with the first lesson, the one that took me three years after my mission to fully understand…

One more thing before we begin.

These lessons didn't change my mission because someone explained them well. They changed my mission because I finally loved the Savior enough to care.

Not love in the abstract, "I know He died for me" way, but real love. The kind that grows when you're far from home, struggling with the language, and He shows up anyway.

That love is what makes everything in this book stick.

If you're not there yet, that's okay. I wasn't either when I got on the plane.

But watch for the moment when that love starts to grow.

Because when it does, these lessons won't feel like advice anymore, they'll feel like confirmation of something you're already beginning to understand.

HOW TO USE THIS BOOK

These five lessons are for missionaries, but you don't have to wait until you receive your mission call.

If you're in middle school or high school right now, these lessons apply to your life today. The principles don't change just because you're not wearing a name tag.

The Savior's love works the same way at fourteen as it does at nineteen. The power of prayer doesn't require a white shirt and tie.

Learning to trust where God has placed you is just as hard in tenth grade as it is in your third transfer.

The difference is that on a mission, life slows down enough to force you to confront these things. Before your mission, it's easier to avoid them.

Life is busy with school, friends, sports, games, and social media. The noise is loud, but the urgency feels low.

What I wish someone had told me at sixteen: the missionaries who thrive are almost always the ones who started learning these lessons before they left.

Not because they were perfect, but because they had already started asking the right questions.

So wherever you are right now, use this book.

If You're in Middle School or High School

- *"I feel like nobody really sees me or knows who I am."* → Go to Chapter 4

- *"I'm stuck somewhere I don't want to be, a school, a town, or a family situation, and I don't understand why."* → Go to Chapter 2

- *"I feel like nothing I do makes a difference."* → Go to Chapter 1

- *"I keep getting distracted from the things I actually care about."* → Go to Chapter 3

- *"I feel pressure to perform and prove myself at school, at church, or in my family."* → Go to Chapter 5

If You're Preparing for a Mission

- *"I'm nervous about where I'll be called and whether I can handle it."* → Go to Chapter 2

- *"I want to understand what missionary work is really about before I leave."* → Go to Chapter 5, then read the rest

- *"I'm worried I'm not spiritual enough or prepared enough."* → Go to Chapter 4

If You're Already Serving

- *"I feel alone, forgotten, or like the Lord doesn't care about me."* → Go to Chapter 4

- *"I'm frustrated with my mission call or where I was sent."* → Go to Chapter 2

- *"I'm discouraged because I'm not seeing baptisms, and I feel like I'm failing."* → Go to Chapters 1 and 5 (read them back-to-back)

- *"I'm exhausted and struggling to find the motivation to keep going."* → Go to Chapter 3

- *"I don't know if what I'm doing even matters."* → Go to Chapter 1

If You're a Recently Returned Missionary

These lessons don't stop applying when you come home. The principles of trusting God's placement, keeping the Savior as your focus, and measuring success by something deeper than visible results will guide you in your career, marriage, parenting, and every calling you undertake.

You'll see yourself in these pages differently now than you did before you left.

Honestly, none of this will matter until you want it to.

Heck, I wouldn't have listened as a teenager.

These lessons landed for me because I was struggling and desperate enough to finally pay attention.

If life is good right now and you're reading this out of obligation, that's okay. Bookmark it. Come back when you need it.

The Lord has a way of creating the moment when this becomes exactly what you were looking for.

CHAPTER 1

YOU NEVER KNOW WHO YOU WILL TOUCH

Why your quiet efforts matter more than visible "results."

And if it so be that you should labor all your days in crying repentance unto this people, and bring, save it be one soul unto me, how great shall be your joy with him in the kingdom of my Father! And now, if your joy will be great with one soul that you have brought unto me into the kingdom of my Father, how great will be your joy if you should bring many souls unto me!

Doctrine and Covenants 18:15–16

Japanese Kotowaza
一期一会 (Ichi-go ichi-e)
"One encounter, one opportunity."

(Every encounter is unique and will never recur in the same way,

treasure each moment and person.)

The Lesson I Learned Three Years Too Late

I didn't learn this lesson until three years after I returned home.

Before I got married, my friend John and I had the chance to go back to Japan. Someone found $500 courier tickets to fly somewhere overseas, fly cheap, and we jumped at the opportunity.

Being back was incredible. I was able to visit people I had grown to love.

Sister Suzuki was a stake missionary in Taniyama, my last area. We had grown very close. I still carry the image of her chasing my bus for three blocks when I left for home, tears streaming down both our faces.

Then there were two sisters I had taught in Nobeoka. They had been furious when a family member joined the Church and left on a mission. But one sister's heart softened, and she agreed to be baptized while I was there. A year after I returned home, the other sister called to tell me she had made the same decision.

We attended church with them in a small branch on the east side of Kyushu.

Walking into that chapel felt surreal, so different from the large home where we had met as missionaries.

Sitting in the congregation were people I had taught. People I had baptized. People who were still… coming to church, still partaking of the sacrament, still living the gospel they had embraced years earlier.

For a returned missionary, there is no greater joy than seeing the people you taught continuing in the faith.

The Woman I Didn't Remember

After the meeting, people came to greet me.

Some I recognized immediately. Others took a moment before the memories came flooding back.

Then a young woman approached me.

"Are you Elder Smith?" she asked in Japanese.

"Yes," I said, searching her face. Had I taught her? Had she been a member when I served here? Nothing came to mind.

She could tell from my expression that I had no idea who she was.

She smiled, almost apologetically. "I didn't think you would remember me," she said.

"But three years ago, you were the first missionary to knock on my door."

She paused, then added words I will never forget:

"I was just baptized a month ago."

Joy, disbelief, and guilt hit me all at once. I had completely forgotten her.

I wanted to shout from the rooftops, but the emotion overwhelmed me, and I could hardly speak.

I don't remember what I said. I would have hugged her, but Japanese culture doesn't embrace that kind of physical contact. I stood there in shock.

We talked for a few minutes, trying to piece together the circumstances. As she described where she lived, the memory slowly surfaced.

My companion and I had knocked on her door one afternoon. She had two small children, a boy and a girl, both under ten.

While my companion spoke with her at the door, I played with her children outside in the hallway.

That was it.

One visit. One brief conversation I wasn't even part of.

Then I was transferred to another area. I never saw her again. Never followed up. Never learned what happened.

I didn't even remember her.

Until that moment, three years later, standing in a chapel in Japan, when she told me she had just come up from the waters of baptism.

The Mistake Many Missionaries Make

When you're serving a mission, you want to see results.

Mission leaders call weekly, asking for numbers.

Don't get me wrong, mission goals matter. Working hard, setting goals, and striving to help people come unto Christ through baptism are all important.

However, goals are meant to motivate you, not define you. They are meant to focus your efforts, not measure your worth.

You can hit every goal and still miss the point if you're not focused on loving people and following the Spirit.

And you can fall short of every numerical target and still have a successful mission if you are faithful, hardworking, and centered on the Savior.

Success isn't measured by hitting numbers. The real goal is to become like Christ through your service.

Yes, you want baptisms. Baptism is an essential ordinance, a gateway to the covenant path.

You want people to accept the message right away, to have powerful conversion experiences during the first discussion, to commit to baptism by the second visit.

I get it. I felt the same way. That's how "success" is sometimes wrongly measured.

But that's not usually how it works.

Most of the time, missionary work feels like planting seeds.

You knock on doors, and people say no.

You teach friends who stop progressing.

You spend weeks with someone who seems interested, only to have them disappear.

You leave an area without seeing a single baptism and wonder if you accomplished anything at all.

I taught many people on my mission who were never baptized while I was there. I've often wondered if they ever were.

Sometimes we are the planters.

Sometimes we are the cultivators.

Sometimes we are the harvesters.

Most of the time, you won't know which role you played.

But the Lord does.

And that person does.

What I Didn't Understand Then

I wasn't the one who baptized that woman in Japan. I was just the first link in a long chain.

It took three years.

Three years of other missionaries knocking on her door. Three years of lessons, conversations, promptings, and invitations. Three years of the Spirit working on her heart.

I played one small part in that process.

I knocked on a door.

That's all.

But it mattered.

That first contact mattered. That moment of showing interest in her family, of being kind to her children, of planting the smallest seed, it all mattered.

The truth is, many missionaries will never receive the kind of confirmation I experienced that day.

Most will go home without seeing the full picture of who they touched.

Some will wonder if any of it mattered.

But the Lord knows.

And He doesn't waste your service.

President Thomas S. Monson taught:

You are making those small acts every day, acts that might not make sense now or bear fruit for years, but acts that matter eternally.

The Biblical Pattern

This isn't just a modern principle. It has been God's pattern from the beginning.

In *1 Corinthians 3*, Paul addresses division in the Church. Some people were saying, "I follow Paul!" Others were saying, "I follow Apollos!"

Paul's response sets ego aside:

"Who then is Paul, and who is Apollos, but ministers by whom ye believed... I have planted, Apollos watered; but God gave the increase.

So then neither is he that planteth anything, neither he that watereth; but God that giveth the increase." (1 Corinthians 3:5–7)

Read that last part again:

"Neither is he that planteth anything, neither he that watereth; but God that giveth the increase."

28

Paul planted.

Apollos watered.

God gave the increase.

You might be the planter.

You might be the one who waters.

You might be the one who harvests.

But you are not God.

You don't control the growth.

Your job is to be faithful in whatever role He gives you in that person's journey.

After years of missionary work among the Lamanites, Ammon reflected on what they had accomplished. But notice his language:

And we have entered into their houses and taught them, and we have taught them in their streets; yea, and we have taught them upon their hills; and we have also entered into their temples and their synagogues and taught them; and we have been cast out, and mocked, and spit upon, and smit upon our cheeks; and we have been stoned, and taken and bound with strong cords, and cast into prison "...we have suffered all manner of afflictions, and all this, that perhaps we might be the means of saving some soul." (Alma 26:29–30)

Did you catch that word?

Perhaps.

Maybe. Possibly.

Even after all that sacrifice, the mockery, the stones, the prison, Ammon doesn't presume success. He knows they were faithful.

And that was enough.

For unto such shall ye continue to minister; for ye know not but when they will return and repent; and come unto me with full purpose of heart, and I shall heal them; and ye shall be the means of salvation unto them. (3 Nephi 18:32)

What This Looks Like on Your Mission

Whether you are preparing or already serving, here is the truth:

Your mission's success is not measured by the number of baptisms.

I know that's hard to hear.

I know mission culture often revolves around numbers, baptism goals, and zone competitions.

I know you will feel pressure to produce results.

But the results are not yours to produce.

Your job is to:

- Reach out to people the way He leads you. In my day, that meant knocking on doors. Today, it might mean a conversation on a train, a connection at a community event, a referral from a member, or a message online. The method has changed, but the mission has not.

- Teach the people He places in your path.

- Love everyone you meet and show that love in the way they need to receive it.

- Plant seeds faithfully.

- Trust Him with the harvest.

- Trust Him as He guides you through every phase of the conversion process.

Some of those seeds will sprout while you are there. Celebrate that. It's a tender mercy.

But many won't.

And that doesn't mean you failed.

Baptisms are not the measure of your faithfulness.

Work hard. Stay worthy so you can teach with power. Invite people to be baptized.

But leave the outcome to God.

The woman in Japan didn't get baptized because I was there. She was baptized because the Lord had been working on her heart for three years through multiple missionaries.

Your job is to be faithful in your part of that process.

At the end of the day, ask yourself:

- Did I work hard?
- Did I love the people?
- Did I teach truth?
- Did I follow the Spirit?

If the answer is yes, you had a successful day, regardless of whether anyone committed to baptism or even listened.

You have no idea who the Lord is preparing.

The person who slams the door today might be baptized five years later because you smiled at them.

The family that says no today might say yes to the next set of missionaries because you were kind.

Treat everyone like they matter.

Because they do.

Playing with someone's children while your companion teaches might feel like you're not contributing, but that moment of kindness could be what they remember years later when deciding whether to meet with missionaries again.

The small things matter.

Be present.

Be kind.

Be genuine.

God's timetable is not your timetable, and that's hard to accept.

The seed you plant today might not sprout until long after you've gone home. That's okay.

Your job is to plant, not to control the growth.

The Lord doesn't need your mission to be statistically impressive.

He needs it to be spiritually faithful.

He's not keeping a scorecard.

He's not comparing your numbers to other missionaries.

He's not disappointed when someone, exercising their agency, chooses not to commit.

He's watching to see if you will:

- Love people even when it's inconvenient.

- Knock on the door, even when it feels pointless.

- Plant seeds, even when you may never see them grow.

- Serve faithfully, even when no one notices.

That's the kind of missionary He's looking for.

There is a kind of joy in missionary work that no one can take from you.

I will never forget the joy I felt that Sunday in Japan.

Standing in that chapel, listening to that young woman tell me she had been baptized, realizing that one simple afternoon three years earlier had mattered, it's a feeling words can't capture.

Thirty years later, I still tear up.

But that joy isn't about me.

It's not about what I did.

It's about what the Lord did, through a chain of faithful missionaries and members who each played their part.

I was lucky enough to see one result. Many missionaries won't.

But the joy of knowing you were faithful, the joy of knowing you loved people, taught truth, and served with your whole heart, whether or not you ever saw the results.

That joy is available to every missionary.

Regardless of baptism numbers.

That's the joy no one can take from you.

A Promise

I promise you this:

Your mission matters, no matter how long you serve.

Every door you knock on matters.

Every person you talk to matters.

Every seed you plant matters.

You might not see it.

You probably won't know about most of it.

But the Lord knows.

And one day, you will understand the full impact of your service.

Until then:

Work hard.

Love everyone.

Plant seeds faithfully.

And trust that God never wastes your service.

His Work, His Way

This isn't your work. It's His.

The Savior spent three years teaching, healing, and loving people. He knew most would reject Him. He knew even His closest disciples would scatter.

He knew that of the thousands who followed Him for bread and miracles, only a handful would remain at the cross.

But He loved them anyway.

He taught them anyway.

He served them anyway.

Not because He needed to see immediate results, but because every single soul mattered to Him.

That's the example He has given you.

Love people, not because you will see them baptized, but because they matter to Him.

Teach truth, not to pad your statistics, but because He has asked you to.

Plant seeds, not to take credit for the harvest, but because you trust Him to bring the increase.

You are His hands. His voice. His representative.

And just as He did, you will plant seeds in hearts you may never see open.

You will teach people who may not accept the message while you are there.

You will love people who may not even remember your name.

But He will remember.

He will see.

He will know every person you touched in His name.

So teach as He taught.

Love as He loved.

Serve as He served.

And trust Him with everything else.

A Final Thought

I served my mission over thirty years ago. Today, I am married with four children, living a life I never could have imagined as a young missionary.

But that moment in Japan, standing in that chapel, hearing that woman's story, and feeling the overwhelming joy of knowing I played a small part in her journey to Christ, remains one of the most powerful spiritual experiences of my life.

Not because I did something great.

But because I was reminded that God can use anyone willing to be used.

Even a young missionary who didn't want to be in Japan. Who went for the wrong reasons.

God used me anyway.

And He will use you too.

You never know who you are really reaching.

So reach out, and love everyone.

For You to Ponder and Act

- Think of someone from your mission or calling who didn't respond the way you hoped. Write their name down. Then pray specifically for them this week, ask the Lord to help that person move further along the covenant path.

For Parents and Leaders

- When you ask someone about their mission or calling, what is the first thing you say? "How are you doing?" or "How many baptisms did you have?" One question shows you care about them. The other suggests you care about their numbers. Make sure they know which one matters more to you.

- Tell one missionary, youth, or ward member a specific way their faithfulness, independent of outcomes, has strengthened your testimony.

Before You Leave

You don't have to be a missionary to plant seeds.

Every conversation with a friend, a teammate, or someone sitting next to you in class is a version of the same principle.

You won't always know what your kindness, your example, or your simple decency does in someone else's life.

Most of the time, you'll never find out.

That's not a reason to stop.

The Lord keeps track of the seeds you plant long before you ever wear a name tag.

Start planting now.

CHAPTER 2

TRUST THE CALL

Seeing God's purpose in every area, transfer, and companion.

Trust in the Lord with all thine heart; and lean not unto thine own understanding. In all thy ways acknowledge him, and he shall direct thy paths.

Proverbs 3:5–6

Japanese Kotowaza

適材適所 (Tekizai tekisho)

"The right person in the right place."

(Everything and everyone has a purpose in the place they are assigned.)

I hate seafood.

Always have. Still do.

So naturally, God assigned me to a place where fish is a dietary staple.

When I opened my mission call and read *"Fukuoka, Japan,"* my first thought wasn't about teaching the gospel or serving the Lord.

It was about surviving two years without eating fish.

Brilliant planning, right? Ask me how that worked out.

Looking back now, I can see the Lord's hand in every single area I served.

But at the time?

I was clueless, frustrated, and confused, wondering why the Lord was sending me to a place that made no sense.

It wasn't until years after my mission, when I finally had time to step back and reflect, that I began to understand why I had been sent to each area.

And when I did, the clarity was stunning.

Every. Single. Area. Had a specific purpose.

Some areas centered on one person accepting baptism. Others taught me patience.

Still others had nothing to do with those we were teaching; they were about helping struggling missionaries.

The problem was, I couldn't see any of it while I was living it.

And that's exactly the point.

The Pattern: Jonah's Problem, and Mine

This struggle isn't new. People have been questioning God's assignments since the beginning.

God called Jonah to preach repentance to Nineveh.

Jonah's response?

"No thanks."

So he boarded a ship going in the opposite direction.

Bad move.

After being thrown overboard, swallowed by a great fish, and spending three days in what had to be the worst Airbnb ever, Jonah finally agreed to go where the Lord sent him.

And you know what happened?

Nineveh repented.

The whole city.

One of the greatest missionary success stories in all of scripture.

Here's what gets me about Jonah's story:

Even after watching an entire city turn to God, Jonah was still upset about it.

He sat outside the city walls, angry that God had shown mercy to people he thought didn't deserve it.

The Lord had to teach him one final lesson:

"Should not I spare Nineveh, that great city?"

Jonah went where he was sent.

He did the work.

But he didn't fully understand why until the Lord taught him about His love for all His children.

I was a lot like Jonah.

I went where I was sent (eventually).

I did the work (mostly).

But I spent far too much time questioning why instead of trusting that the Lord knew exactly what He was doing.

The Girl I Almost Missed

My first area was Kita Kyushu. I was greener than green. I could barely speak the language.

A teenage girl had been meeting with the missionaries for a while. I didn't teach her much. My companion did most of the talking while I sat there trying to understand what anyone was saying.

Then, during one particular lesson, about six months into my time there, I felt something.

A prompting. Clear as day.

Invite her to be baptized.

I hesitated.

I was the junior companion. I could barely speak Japanese. I rehearsed the sentence in my mind over and over, terrified I would say it wrong, or worse, offend her.

What business did I have extending that invitation?

But the feeling wouldn't go away.

So I did it.

In my broken, barely understandable Japanese, I invited her to be baptized.

She said yes.

The next week, I was transferred.

I wasn't there for her baptism. I didn't see her enter the water. I didn't get the "victory" of that moment.

At the time, I was frustrated.

Why send me there if I wasn't going to see the fruits of the work?

Years later, I finally understood.

That was why I was sent to Kita Kyushu.

Not to baptize her myself. Not to receive credit, but to be there at exactly the right moment to extend that invitation when the Spirit prompted.

I was in the right place at the right time, even though I had no idea.

The blessing wasn't in seeing the baptism.

The blessing was in obeying the prompting and trusting the Lord with the results.

When I Lost My Temper

Still in Kita Kyushu, I had a companion who thought it was hilarious to thump my head and flick me throughout the day.

I know. Super mature.

I asked him to stop multiple times.

He didn't.

At first, I laughed it off. Then I tolerated it. Eventually, I started dreading being around him.

I was trying to be patient. Trying to turn the other cheek. Trying to be Christlike.

But if I'm honest, I wasn't being patient at all.

I was bottling up anger and resentment day after day, convincing myself that suffering in silence made me righteous.

One day, I ran out of patience.

We were walking down the hallway of the church building when he thumped my head again.

Something snapped.

I turned around and punched him in the chest.

Not hard enough to hurt him, but hard enough to make a point.

"Don't ever touch me again."

He never did.

I wish I could tell you I handled that situation perfectly.

I didn't.

I let frustration build until it exploded, and I responded with force instead of wisdom.

That's not how the Savior would have handled it.

But I learned something important from that failure.

Patience isn't about being a doormat.

It's not about allowing people to mistreat you while you silently seethe.

Real patience involves honest communication, firm boundaries, and addressing problems before they explode.

I needed to learn that lesson.

And apparently, the only way I was going to learn it was the hard way, by doing it wrong first.

Looking back, I think the Lord sent me to Kita Kyushu partly to break down my pride.

I thought I was more righteous than my companion because I "endured" his behavior.

But pride dressed up as patience is still pride.

The Lord had to teach me that being Christlike doesn't mean being passive.

It means being honest, kind, and firm.

President Ezra Taft Benson taught:

"The Lord works from the inside out. The world works from the outside in. The world would take people out of the slums. Christ takes the slums out of people, and then they take themselves out of the slums."

("Born of God," General Conference, October 1985)

The Lord wasn't just sending me places to teach other people. He was sending me places to change me from the inside out.

Christ's Example: The Perfect Pattern

The Savior knows what it feels like to be sent somewhere hard.

He left His Father's presence to come to earth. He was born in a stable.

He was raised in Nazareth, a place so insignificant that Nathanael asked, *"Can there any good thing come out of Nazareth?"* (John 1:46)

The Savior could have been born in Rome, in a palace.

But He wasn't.

He was born exactly where the Father needed Him to be.

Later, when He faced His greatest trial in Gethsemane, He prayed:

"Father, if thou be willing, remove this cup from me: nevertheless not my will, but thine, be done." (Luke 22:42)

Not my will, but thine.

That's what I should have been praying.

Not, *"Why am I here with this companion?"*

Not, *"This makes no sense!"*

Not, *"Please give me a new assignment."*

It's not about understanding why you are in a particular place.

It's about trusting that the Lord's plan is better than yours.

It's not about feeling qualified or prepared.

It's about being willing to say, *"Not my will, but thine."*

Christ trusted His Father, and because He did, He accomplished the greatest work in all of human history.

Your mission isn't about you.

It's about Him.

About following His example of trust, obedience, and love.

When you make Him the center of your mission, everything else begins to fall into place.

The frustrating companion becomes a teacher.

The difficult area becomes a classroom.

The transfer you don't understand becomes exactly what you needed.

Called to the Work

When you open your mission call, the first lines state that you are called to serve as a full-time missionary and explain what that means. Then you read where you are assigned to labor.

Notice the order:

You are called to serve first.

Then you are taught what that means.

Only after that are you assigned a place.

Elder David A. Bednar taught:

"A missionary is not called to a place; rather, he or she is called to serve."

("Called to Serve," General Conference, April 2017)

Your calling is to represent the Savior.

So when you feel frustrated about where you are serving. When you compare your assignment to someone else's. When things don't go the way you expected.

Remember:

You weren't called to Japan, or Peru, or Tennessee.

You were called to be the Savior's representative.

The assignment to a specific place is secondary to that sacred calling.

Years after my mission, I had the blessing of serving as a bishop.

One of the young women in my ward decided to serve a mission. I knew her well, She was faithful, talented; the kind of missionary any mission president would be thrilled to have.

We worked through the paperwork and interviews, and she soon received her mission call.

A stateside mission.

A few days after she opened her call, she came to see me on a Sunday afternoon, dejected and discouraged.

"Bishop, do you really think mission calls are inspired?" she asked.

I didn't hesitate.

"Absolutely."

She said, "Okay," and left still sad. But she moved forward and prepared to serve.

And she became a wonderful missionary.

She served faithfully and gave her best.

A few days after she returned home, we had a quiet moment together.

I reminded her of the question she had asked me after receiving her call.

Then I said, "Let me ask you a question."

She smiled, knowing what was coming.

"Are mission calls inspired?" I asked.

A smile…

Followed by tears.

"Yes, Bishop. They are inspired."

The Lord had sent her exactly where she needed to be.

She couldn't see it at first, just as I couldn't when I received my call to Japan. But over time, she came to understand that she had been placed there for a reason.

The pattern repeats itself, generation after generation.

Young missionaries open their calls and find themselves staring at a place they didn't expect, in a country they didn't choose, facing food they don't like.

They wonder why.

They question.

Some even struggle with their faith, wondering if the Lord truly knows what He is doing.

But the answer is always the same:

Yes.

The call is inspired.

You just can't see it yet.

You are where you are for such a time as this.

Not by accident.

Not by mistake.

But because the Lord knew you needed to be there.

Just like Esther, who found herself in an impossible position as queen of Persia when a plot emerged to destroy her people.

Her cousin Mordecai sent her a message that speaks to every missionary:

"Who knoweth whether thou art come to the kingdom for such a time as this?" (Esther 4:14)

You are where you are, for such a time as this.

Through inspiration, a prophet of God issued your call.

And the Lord, through your mission president, will send you where He needs you.

President Thomas S. Monson taught:

> *"Whom the Lord calls, the Lord qualifies."*
> *("We Are Not Alone," General Conference, April 2010)*

But I'd add this: whom the Lord calls, the Lord sends to exactly the right place.

Not the place YOU think you should be. The place HE knows you need to be.

Maybe it's to teach one specific person. Maybe it's to learn a hard lesson about yourself. Maybe it's to help another missionary who's struggling.

Or maybe, as it was for me in several of my areas, it's all of the above.

You don't need to understand everything right now. You just need to be faithful and patient, trusting that the fruit will come in the Lord's timing.

How They Met Me Where I Was

I didn't know it when I opened my mission call, but Fukuoka, Japan, was exactly the right mission for me.

President Cyril Figuerres had spent years studying how to foster real spiritual growth in Japan. Under Elder Neal A. Maxwell's direction, he developed the Ammon Project, which taught us how to minister to and serve non-Christian Japanese people.

The goal was simple: help people come to Christ by loving them regardless of their readiness and by helping them feel the Holy Spirit.

Because the Spirit converts.

Not the missionary.

Not the methods.

Not the discussions.

Here's what mattered most:

President and Sister Figuerres loved me exactly where I was, without judgment.

They didn't shame me for going on my mission for the wrong reasons.

They mentored me.

They showed me what it looked like to serve the way the Savior served.

Thirty years later, they still mentor me. They still love me.

I am eternally grateful my Heavenly Father placed me exactly where I needed to be.

What This Means for You Right Now

So, how do you actually live this?

How do you trust your call when the work is hard, the area feels fruitless, and your companion is testing every ounce of patience you have?

Here's what I wish someone had told me:

Stop Asking "Why Am I Here?"

Don't go into each area thinking, *"What does the Lord want me to do here?"*

And definitely don't go in thinking, *"Why am I here?"*

Both questions can put you in the wrong mindset.

They cause you to obsess over finding some grand purpose instead of simply doing the work.

Work hard.

Love the people.

Serve with your whole heart.

The "why" will come later when you have time to reflect.

Pray Different Prayers

Instead of praying, *"Please give me a new companion"* or *"Please transfer me out of here,"* pray what Christ prayed:

"Not my will, but thine."

"Help me see what You see."

"Help me love who You love."

Those prayers change you.

Look for the Lessons, Not Just the Results

In some areas, you will see baptisms. In others, you won't.

Some companions will become lifelong friends. Others will test you to your core.

All of them are teaching you something.

Pay attention to what you are learning about yourself, about the gospel, and about the Savior.

Each ordinance matters eternally to the person receiving it.

But what are you learning in that moment?

That may be exactly why the Lord sent you there.

Trust the process.

The Lord is not making mistakes with your assignments.

He is not randomly moving missionaries around, hoping something works out.

He knows exactly what He is doing.

Your job is to trust Him and do your best.

Remember Who You're Following

When you feel frustrated…

When the area feels fruitless…

When the transfer doesn't make sense…

When you feel like giving up

Remember:

The Savior was sent to earth when He could have remained in glory.
He was born in a stable when He deserved a palace. He went to Gethsemane when every part of Him wanted to turn away.

And still, He said:

"Not my will, but thine."

If He could trust the Father's plan even when it led to the cross, you can trust it too.

Even when it leads you somewhere uncomfortable.

Even if that place happens to serve fish for breakfast, lunch, and dinner.

A Final Thought

Remember the Japanese *kotowaza* at the beginning of this chapter?

適材適所 (*Tekizai tekisho*) "The right person in the right place."

That's you.

Right now.

Wherever you are.

You might be in your first area, feeling lost, unsure why you're there, with a companion who drives you crazy.

But you are exactly where you need to be.

Not because the place is perfect, but because the Lord sent you there for a reason.

He doesn't make mistakes.

I promise you, one day you will look back and see it clearly.

The Lord knew exactly what He was doing.

He always does.

For You to Ponder and Act

- Think about a time you were placed somewhere you didn't choose or didn't understand, an area, a companion, a difficult season of your mission, or even where you are right now. Write down one specific way the Lord might be using it to change you from the inside out.

- In your prayer today, say: *"Father, I don't fully understand why Thou placed me here, but I choose to trust Thee."*

For Parents and Leaders

- Share a story of a calling, assignment, or difficult season that only made sense afterward, and how you came to see the Lord's hand in it.

Before You Leave

You have already been sent somewhere.

The school you didn't choose.

The town your family moved you to.

The team with the coach you can't stand.

The Lord has been placing you in the right place at the right time your entire life.

You just haven't had enough distance to see it yet.

The next time you find yourself somewhere you don't want to be, ask a different question.

Instead of *"Why am I here?"* try:

"What is here for me?"

The answer may come later.

But it will come.

CHAPTER 3

KEEP THE SAVIOR'S LIFE AND MINISTRY AS YOUR FOCUS

Letting Christ, not numbers, define the way you serve.

But seek ye first the kingdom of God, and his righteousness; and all these things shall be added unto you.

Matthew 6:33

Japanese Kotowaza
初心忘るべからず *(Shoshin wasuru bekarazu)*
"Never forget your original intention."

(Even as you gain experience, don't lose sight of your original purpose,

why you started in the first place.)

It Can't Be Morning Already

I woke one morning to the alarm clock blaring.

I was exhausted, not just physically, but mentally drained.

Had I gotten any sleep at all?

It didn't feel like it.

Every part of me wanted to hit snooze and steal a few more hours.

As I lay there, struggling to get up, words from a song by Kenneth Cope, *"Never a Greater Hero"*, echoed in my mind:

"Not one regret, true to the end."

I had heard that song countless times, but those words had never hit me the way they did that morning.

The Savior knew how His earthly ministry would end, that He would be lifted up on the cross.

And still, He carried on. He pressed forward. He served those around Him.

He never looked for a way out. He never gave up.

"Not one regret, true to the end."

I was only weeks away from going home.

I thought about my Savior and all He had done for me.

If He could carry the weight of the world and never quit, I could get out of bed.

If my Savior, knowing what awaited Him, could press forward…

With His strength, so could I.

That was all the motivation I needed.

I got up and got back to work.

From that day on, whenever I struggled to get moving, those words returned, and so did the desire to press forward.

That was the moment I began to understand what this lesson is really about.

It's not about working harder.

It's not about being more obedient.

It's not about trying to be perfect.

It's about keeping your eyes on Him when everything else is trying to pull your focus away.

The Numbers Trap

I was asked to speak at the zone conference about mission goals.

The problem?

We had been grinding through those goals every week, often doubling them, and still weren't seeing the promised results.

How was I supposed to stand up and testify about something I couldn't see working?

I agonized over it for days.

Then, a few days before the zone conference, a thought came:

Look at your actual numbers over time.

Reluctantly, I pulled out my weekly reports.

I tallied everything: every contact, every lesson, every commitment, every baptism.

And I was shocked.

I had been so focused on the weeks when nothing happened that I completely missed what God had been doing over time.

When I averaged the baptisms across the entire period, we were hitting exactly what had been promised.

Some months, we saw nothing.

Then three baptisms the next month.

The framework had worked perfectly.

I just couldn't see it because I was obsessed with the timing instead of trusting the Lord.

I had become so focused on *when* baptisms should happen that I stopped seeing the people.

I had turned people into statistics.

Let me explain what I had missed:

President Figuerres had given us a statistical framework based on research he had done in Japan.

He wasn't trying to create baptism quotas.

He was trying to help us avoid a trap that many missionaries fall into.

The trap?

Setting impossibly high goals…

Failing month after month…

And quietly concluding that you are a terrible missionary.

So you keep going through the motions.

You don't tell your mission president you've given up.

You just keep knocking on doors, smiling, and pretending, so no one thinks you failed.

He didn't want that for us.

He wanted us to have realistic expectations and achievable goals, so we wouldn't burn out.

I had made it about numbers instead of people.

About performance instead of conversion.

About *my timeline* instead of the Lord's.

What I should have understood was this:

The goal isn't baptism numbers.

The goal is to help people truly come unto Christ.

Helping them change intellectually, spiritually, emotionally, and behaviorally.

Helping them become united in love with members of their local ward or branch.

That's the work.

Baptism?

That is the sacred *byproduct* of genuine conversion to Jesus Christ.

When someone truly becomes converted to Him, they will want to be baptized.

Let me be clear:

Baptismal covenants are essential.

Making and keeping covenants is central to eternal life.

Baptism is a sacred moment when someone chooses to bind themselves to God.

This isn't about saying baptisms don't matter.

It's about understanding that baptism numbers should not be your primary focus.

When you focus on helping people feel the Savior's love… When you minister in a way that invites the Spirit into every interaction…
When you are motivated by love and guided by the Spirit

Baptisms happen.

Not always when you expect.

Not always on your timeline.

Not always while you are there (see Lesson 1).

But they happen.

When you obsess over numbers, you stop seeing people.

But when you keep your focus on the Savior, on how He loved, taught, and ministered

The numbers take care of themselves.

Peter Walking on the Water

One of my favorite stories in the Bible is Peter walking on water.

The disciples were out in a boat, caught in a storm, struggling through the night.

They must have been exhausted, wet, cold, and miserable.

Then they saw something in the distance.

Someone… or something… walking on the water toward them.

A ghost? What was it?

Fear set in

Until they heard a familiar voice:

"Be of good cheer; it is I; be not afraid." (Matthew 14:27)

Peter, recognizing his Master, said:

"Lord, if it be thou, bid me come unto thee on the water." *(Matthew 14:28)*

And Jesus replied as He always does:

"Come."

Peter stepped out of the boat.

For a moment, he did the impossible.

He walked on water.

But then, he took his eyes off Jesus.

He noticed the wind.

The waves.

The storm around him.

And he began to sink.

"Lord, save me!" he cried.

Immediately, Jesus reached out and caught him.

"O thou of little faith, wherefore didst thou doubt?" *(Matthew 14:31)*

We often stop the story there.

But the next part matters just as much.

Jesus walked back to the boat with Peter.

And when they reached the boat, the wind ceased.

Which means the storm continued the entire way back.

There's a lesson in that.

This story perfectly illustrates why we must keep our eyes on the Savior.

Not just during your mission, but through all of life's storms.

As long as Peter kept his focus on Christ, he could do the impossible.

The moment he focused on the storm of fear, on circumstances, he began to sink.

Your mission will have storms.

Plenty of them.

Friends who won't progress.

Companions who frustrate you.

Days when nothing seems to work.

Weeks when you feel like you're failing.

In those moments, you have a choice:

Focus on Christ, or focus on the storm.

If you focus on the storm, you will sink.

But if you keep your focus on Him, on His example, on His love for people, you can do the impossible.

And even when you do take your eyes off Him as we all do sometimes and begin to sink…

He is still there.

Ready to catch you.

Ready to lift you.

Ready to walk with you through the storm.

That's the Savior I came to know on my mission.

The One who doesn't abandon you when you struggle.

The One who reaches out, lifts you up, and walks beside you until you're safe.

When Jesus Ministered

What did Christ's focus actually look like?

How did He minister during His time on earth?

He didn't rush.

He didn't stress about numbers.

He didn't treat people like projects.

He saw people.

Think about the woman at the well.

Jesus was tired. He had been traveling. His disciples had gone to buy food.

He could have rested.

Instead, He chose to stop.

To talk with a Samaritan woman, an outcast. Someone no respectable Jewish rabbi would normally speak to.

He asked her for water.

He started a conversation.

He taught her about living water.

Because of that one moment, many Samaritans believed.

Not because He was trying to meet a goal

But because He saw her.

Really saw her.

Loved her.

And taught her truth.

Or consider Zacchaeus.

A tax collector. Despised. Seen as a traitor.

He climbed a tree just to catch a glimpse of Jesus.

Jesus could have walked right past him.

Instead, He stopped.

He looked up.

He called him by name.

And invited Himself to Zacchaeus's home.

That one moment changed Zacchaeus's life forever.

That's how Jesus ministered.

One person at a time.

With love.

Without judgment.

Focused on individuals, not outcomes.

When you follow His example, missionary work stops being about numbers

And starts being about people.

That's what Christ's focus looks like.

He saw people.

Really saw them.

Loved them.

Met them where they were.

I wish I could tell you I learned this lesson on my mission and never forgot it.

But years later, as a bishop…

I forgot.

When I Forgot What the Savior Would Do

I had only been serving as a bishop for a few months when the email arrived.

My son was serving a mission in Ghana, and his message read:

"Bishop, we need to talk."

Never a good email to receive, especially from your own son.

He had some things he needed to work through.

He was coming home early.

To say I was upset would be a massive understatement.

I was angry.

Not just disappointed, angry in a way I hadn't expected.

Embarrassed. Defensive. Worried about what people would think.

My first reaction wasn't Christlike.

I cared more about how it looked than about what my son actually needed.

And if I'm being completely honest…

I was mad at God.

Think about that for a second.

A bishop, angry with God.

Not exactly a great place to be spiritually.

For the previous five years, I had served on the high council with responsibility for youth programs in our stake.

I poured everything I had into that calling.

I loved those youth. I did everything I could to help them feel the Savior's love.

And now my own son was coming home early from his mission?

My thinking, twisted as it was, went something like this:

"Really, God? I spent five years doing everything you asked. I gave everything I had to those youth… and THIS is what I get?"

Yeah.

I was in a great place spiritually.

While my son was on the plane heading home, my father-in-law came over.

He sat down across from me and said:

"I want you to be completely honest with me. Who does your son need right now?"

I assumed he was looking for the "right" answer.

So I said, "He needs his dad."

"Okay," he replied. "Now, be really honest. As his dad, what do you want to do when he walks through that door?"

I paused. If I were being completely honest.

I wanted to take him behind the woodshed and make it very clear how much he had embarrassed our family.

How messed up is that?

My father-in-law thanked me for being honest.

Then he asked one more question:

"If this were any other youth in your ward coming home early, what would you do as their bishop?"

The answer came instantly.

I knew exactly what I would do.

I would put my arm around them.

I would tell them I loved them.

I would remind them that their worth was not tied to how long they served or whether they "completed" a mission.

Then he looked me straight in the eyes and said something I will never forget:

"Your son needs his bishop."

That moment changed me.

Not just as a father.

Not just as a bishop.

But in how I have tried to serve ever since.

I had completely lost sight of what Jesus would do.

I was so wrapped up in my own embarrassment… my pride… my hurt…

That I forgot the most important question:

What would the Savior do?

The woman at the well was an outcast.

He saw her. Loved her. Changed her life.

Zacchaeus, a traitor in everyone's eyes.

Jesus stopped. Called him by name. Invited Himself to dinner.

My son is coming home early.

Embarrassed. Afraid.

What would Jesus do?

He wouldn't lecture.

He wouldn't shame.

He wouldn't focus on how it looked to other people.

He would simply love.

President Thomas S. Monson taught:

"Never let a problem to be solved become more important than a person to be loved." ("Finding Joy in the Journey," General Conference, October 2008)

I had turned my son into a problem to solve instead of a person to love.

As a missionary, you will face moments when it's easy to lose sight of Christ's example.

Maybe someone you're teaching breaks a commitment for the fourth time.

Maybe your companion frustrates you.

Maybe you feel like you're working harder than everyone else and getting nowhere.

In those moments, remember this:

The work isn't about you.

It's not about your success, your reputation, or your numbers.

It's about following Christ's example, loving people right where they are.

When you keep His life and ministry as your focus, things begin to align with His will.

But when you lose that focus even briefly, you end up as I did:

Sitting in your living room, frustrated… even angry… because things didn't go the way *you* expected.

Keep your eyes on Him.

Always.

Practical Application

So what does this actually look like day to day?

Before anything else, spend time with the Savior.

Read about His life.

Study how He served.

Pray to become more like Him.

Don't just pray for success.

Pray for charity.

Pray to be filled with His love so you can share it with others.

When You Face Challenges

Ask yourself:

What would Jesus do?

Yes, it may sound simple. But it becomes powerful when you truly mean it.

When someone cancels again, what would Jesus do? He would love them anyway.

When your companion frustrates you, what would Jesus do? He would be patient. Kind. Willing to serve.

When you feel discouraged about your numbers, what would Jesus do?
He would refocus on the one.

Remember: "The Goal" Isn't the Goal

Yes, set goals.

Yes, work toward them.

Follow the inspired direction of your mission leaders.

But don't let goals become your focus.

The goal isn't to hit numbers.

The goal is to become like Christ while you serve to help others feel His love and to guide them toward Him and the covenant path.

Measure your day by this:

Did I love people today?

Did I treat them the way Jesus would?

Did I help someone feel His love?

If the answer is yes, you had a successful day.

Regardless of what the numbers say.

When that becomes your focus, the results take care of themselves.

But here's the truth:

You cannot do this on your own.

You cannot become like Christ through willpower alone.

You will fall short.

I did constantly.

The Savior's atoning sacrifice doesn't just forgive you when you fail.

It changes you.

As you honor your covenants, His grace gives you power.

To love when you don't feel like loving.

To be patient when you're frustrated.

To keep going when you're exhausted.

He promised:

"I will not leave you comfortless: I will come to you." (John 14:18)

When you feel alone, He is there.

When you lose focus and begin to sink, He is there, reaching out.

So when you fail to keep your focus on Him

When you get caught up in numbers, pride, or frustration

Don't give up.

Turn back to Him.

Let His grace change you.

Let His love fill you.

Then get up and try again.

A Final Thought

This lesson is simple to say.

But hard to live.

Keep the Savior's life and ministry as your focus in all you do.

Study His words.

Learn from His example.

Ask yourself often: *What would He do?*

You will still have hard days.

You will still struggle.

But He will be your anchor, your example, your source of strength.

Remember the words that echoed in my mind that morning:

"Not one regret, true to the end."

The Savior gave everything.

He held nothing back.

He stayed true to His mission even when it led to the cross.

His promise isn't a life without struggle.

It's something better:

Faithfulness.

Love.

And the assurance that He is with you, every step of the way.

Study His life.

Follow His example.

Keep Him as your focus.

And when you do, your mission becomes what it was always meant to be

Not a test to pass…

But a privilege.

An opportunity to follow in His footsteps.

A joyful one.

…Even if you have to eat fish.

For You to Ponder and Act

- Think about the last time you felt truly focused on the Savior during your service, not on goals or outcomes. What was different? Write it down, and ask the Lord to help you return to that feeling.

- Read one story from Christ's ministry in the Gospels or 3 Nephi. Then complete this sentence:

For Parents and Leaders

- Share your favorite story from the Savior's life, and explain how it has shaped the way you serve.

- Is there someone in your life who needs to hear that representing Jesus Christ matters more than any number or outcome? Find a natural moment to tell them.

Before You Leave

The distractions that will pull your focus from a mission are already pulling at you now.

The difference?

Right now, there are more distractions and fewer reasons to resist them.

Learning to keep the Savior as your anchor *before* you leave is one of the best ways to prepare.

Not by being perfect.

Not by being overly religious.

But by building a simple habit:

When things get hard or confusing, ask:

What would He do here?

Practice that now.

So when you need it most

It's already part of who you are.

CHAPTER 4

DON'T UNDERESTIMATE THE POWER OF PRAYER AND THE LORD'S LOVE FOR YOU

How honest prayer and feeling His love carry you through the hard days.

And when thou prayest, thou shalt not be as the hypocrites are: for they love to pray standing in the synagogues and in the corners of the streets, that they may be seen of men. Verily I say unto you, They have their reward. But thou, when thou prayest, enter into thy closet, and when thou hast shut thy door, pray to thy Father which is in secret; and thy Father which seeth in secret shall reward thee openly.

Matthew 6:5–6

Japanese Kotowaza
石の上にも三年 (Ishi no ue ni mo san nen)
"Three years on a cold stone."

(With patience and persistence, even sitting on a cold stone for three years will warm it. Keep praying, keep trying, keep trusting, even when it feels like nothing is happening.)

Does He Even Love Me?

I was in my first area in Japan. I couldn't speak the language. I was frustrated, frustrated enough to question whether I should even be on a mission.

Was this *really* what the Lord wanted for me? Or had I made a huge mistake?

With only the fragile beginnings of a testimony to hold on to, I was starting to believe it was the latter.

One evening, after another long day, my companion and I returned to our apartment. I went straight into our bedroom and shut the door. I needed to be alone.

I felt isolated and inadequate, far from home and everything familiar.

In that state of mind, I did the only thing I could think of.

I got down on my knees and cried out to my Heavenly Father.

It was the sincerest prayer I had ever offered, far more sincere than the times I had asked for a sign.

I asked the Lord one simple question:

"Do You love me?"

Then I sat in silence and listened.

In that quiet space, it didn't take long before it felt as if someone had walked into the room, gathered me into their arms, and held me.

I don't have the words to fully describe what I felt that night.

But five words came clearly into my mind:

"Elder Smith, I love you."

That was it.

No lecture.

No commandments.

No instruction manual on how to be a better missionary.

Just five simple words.

And in that moment, they were exactly what I needed, exactly what I needed to feel.

The Lord knew what I needed, and He gave it to me.

That love was enough to carry me through the next day.

The Zone Leader Without a Companion

While I was serving as a zone leader in Oita, my companion was called to serve as an assistant to the president.

My new companion wouldn't arrive for a couple of weeks. He needed time to train his replacement in the mission home.

So for a short period, I was leading a zone on my own.

To stay within mission rules, my mission president asked me to rely on members and nearby missionaries for companionship.

One night, I came home feeling completely overwhelmed, alone, and emotionally drained.

It felt like I was drowning, with no lifeline in sight.

Once again, I went into my room, knelt down, and asked the same question:

"Do You love me?"

And just like in my first area, I felt His love.

I didn't suddenly understand *why* I was going through those challenges. Most of the time, we don't.

But one thing became clear:

The Lord loved me.

And knowing that was enough to help me keep going.

Truth in the Middle of Discouragement

President Monson taught:

> *"Each of us should remember that he or she is a son or daughter of God, endowed with faith, gifted with courage, and guided by prayer. Our eternal destiny is before us. At times many of us let that enemy of achievement smother our dreams, cloud our vision, and impair our lives.*
>
> *The enemy's voice whispers in our ears, 'You can't do it.' 'You're too young.' 'You're too old.' 'You're nobody.' This is when we remember that we are created in the*

image of God. Reflection on this truth provides a profound sense of strength and power."

("Be of Good Cheer," General Conference, April 2009)

Read that again. Let it sink in.

Discouragement is one of the adversary's most effective tools. He whispers:

You're not enough.

You're failing.

You don't belong here.

But prayer reminds you of something greater.

It reminds you of who you really are.

A son or daughter of God.

As you honor your covenants, you are endowed with faith, strengthened with courage, and guided by prayer.

The Wrestle Enos Had

Enos went into the woods to hunt. While he was there, the words his father had taught him began to sink deep into his heart.

His soul hungered.

So he knelt down and began to pray.

He prayed all day. Then all night, "wrestling before God."

That's the kind of prayer we're talking about. Not routine words. Not going through the motions. A deep, honest, vulnerable conversation with his Heavenly Father.

After that long wrestle, a voice came to him:

"Enos, thy sins are forgiven thee, and thou shalt be blessed."

Enos later wrote:

"I, Enos, knew that God could not lie; wherefore, my guilt was swept away." (Enos 1:5–6)

That's the power of sincere prayer.

Prayer that brings peace.

Prayer that brings assurance.

Prayer that reminds you that God sees you and loves you.

You will have moments on your mission when you need that kind of prayer. Moments when a quick, casual prayer won't be enough.

Moments when you need to wrestle before God and receive your own answer.

The Brother of Jared's Prayer

The Brother of Jared's story teaches another powerful truth: sometimes prayer doesn't remove the storm, but it gives you the strength to endure it.

His people were preparing to cross the ocean in barges, and they faced two major problems.

First, the barges were "tight like unto a dish," meaning there would be little to no airflow.

Second, because they were completely enclosed, there would be no light.

The Brother of Jared brought these concerns to the Lord.

For the first problem, the Lord gave specific instructions: cut a hole in the top and bottom of each barge. When they needed air, they would open one hole and plug the other.

Think about that for a moment.

If they had to switch the plugs, it means those barges were being flipped upside down… and back again.

For nearly a year.

That doesn't sound like a peaceful journey. It sounds like a year-long lesson in faith and endurance.

Then came the second problem: light.

And this time, the Lord responded differently.

In essence, He asked, *"What do you want me to do?"*

That must have been surprising.

I probably would have said, "You're God, shouldn't You already know?"

But the Brother of Jared didn't hesitate.

He acted.

He carved sixteen stones out of rock, carried them up a mountain, and asked the Lord to touch them to make them shine.

That took faith.

That took effort.

That took initiative.

And that's the lesson:

Prayer is not passive.

It's not just asking God to fix everything.

It's bringing your effort, your ideas, your willingness, and then asking Him to magnify it.

You will face challenges that feel overwhelming. Pray about them. Do your part. Then trust the Lord to do what you cannot.

Even the Savior Prayed

If anyone didn't "need" to pray, it was Jesus Christ.

He was perfect. Sinless. The Son of God.

And yet, He prayed constantly.

Before feeding the five thousand, He prayed.

After long days of teaching and healing, He withdrew to be alone and pray.

In His darkest moment, in the Garden of Gethsemane, He prayed so intensely that He sweat drops of blood.

Prayer wasn't a ritual for Him.

It was His lifeline.

His connection to the Father.

His source of strength.

If the Savior needed prayer, how much more do we?

Thousands Are Praying for You

In temples around the world, during every endowment session, prayers are offered.

And almost always, those prayers include missionaries.

Think about that.

Every temple.

Every session.

All across the world.

Thousands of prayers every single week, asking God to bless and protect you.

Your family is praying for you.

Your leaders are praying for you.

People you may never meet are praying for you.

So when you feel discouraged… when you feel forgotten… when you feel alone

remember this:

You are not alone.

You are surrounded by prayers.

Practical Applications

So, how do you actually apply this as a missionary?

It's easy to let prayer become routine, saying the same things every day without really thinking. Don't let that happen.

Before you pray, pause. Think about what you truly need to say.

When you pray, talk to your Heavenly Father the way you would talk to someone who knows you completely and loves you anyway.

Be honest.

Be vulnerable.

Tell Him how you're really feeling. Ask the hard questions. He can handle it. In fact, He *wants* to hear them.

When you feel discouraged, ask that one simple question:

"Do You love me?"

I promise you, if you ask sincerely, He will answer.

Not always immediately.

Not always in the same way.

But He will answer.

Maybe with words.

Maybe with a feeling.

Maybe with a peace that "passeth all understanding" (Philippians 4:7).

But the answer will come in His time, and in His way.

Pray for the people you teach by name. Ask the Lord to help you understand what they need physically, emotionally, and spiritually. Ask Him to help you see them the way He does.

Ask Him to soften their hearts and yours.

You'll be surprised how much prayer changes the way you feel about people.

Pray for your companion, too.

Whether you get along or not, pray for them. Ask the Lord to help you see them through His eyes. Prayer has a way of softening hearts, and it usually starts with our own.

Consider keeping a prayer journal.

As you pray, take time to pause and listen. When impressions come, write them down.

Over time, you'll begin to see patterns. You'll recognize how the Lord has been guiding you, even when you didn't notice it in the moment.

And on hard days, you'll be able to look back and remember:

He has answered before.

He will answer again.

A Final Thought

You will face struggles as a missionary.

Hard days.

Lonely days.

Days when it feels like nothing you do is making a difference.

In those moments, remember this:

The Lord loves you.

If you ask Him that simple question, He will answer, and that answer will give you the strength to keep going.

Remember the Japanese saying: *"Three years on a cold stone."*

It teaches that real change takes time. Growth often requires more patience and discomfort than we expect.

So keep praying.

Keep trusting.

Keep believing.

Even when it feels like nothing is happening, He is working.

Even when you can't see it, He is there.

He loves you more than you can fully understand.

And who knows… maybe He'll even help you like fish.

Nope. Still didn't work for me.

For You to Ponder and Act

- When was the last time you prayed and actually waited in silence for an answer instead of moving straight to "amen"? Tonight, try it. Ask one honest question, then listen. Write down whatever comes.

- Tonight, tell Heavenly Father one thing you're truly afraid of, ashamed of, or confused about without trying to clean it up first.

For Parents and Leaders

- Think about the last time someone heard you pray with complete honesty instead of polished, "Sunday" language. Would they know from your prayers that God is someone you truly talk to?
- When someone you love is struggling, resist the urge to fix it with advice. Instead, ask if you can kneel and pray with them.

Before You Leave

The prayer I described in this chapter, the one where I asked the Lord if He loved me, was not a "missionary" prayer.

It was a human one.

You don't have to be in Japan to ask it.

You can ask it tonight. In your room. With the door closed.

If you've never had a real, honest, vulnerable conversation with your Heavenly Father, start now.

Not a routine prayer.

A real one.

Tell Him what you're actually feeling. Ask the question you've been afraid to ask.

He can handle it.

And the answer He gives you now will stay with you for the rest of your life on your mission and long after.

CHAPTER 5

BAPTISMS ARE NOT THE FOCUS, THE SAVIOR'S LOVE IS

Helping people feel the Savior's love and recognize His voice.

But the Comforter, which is the Holy Ghost, whom the Father will send in my name, he shall teach you all things, and bring all things to your remembrance, whatsoever I have said unto you.

John 14:26

Japanese Kotowaza
心に響く (Kokoro ni hibiku)
"To resound in the heart."
(When truth strikes the heart, it creates a resonance that cannot

be denied. This is how the Spirit works.)

The Most Important Lesson

If you learn nothing else from this book, let it be this:

Baptisms should not be your focus.

The Spirit should be.

Helping others feel the Savior's love should be.

You might think I've lost my mind or that this is a typo. It's not.

Let me be clear: I am *not* saying baptisms are unimportant. They are essential. They open the gate to the covenant path.

What I'm talking about is obsession.

Here's what might surprise you. *Preach My Gospel* says it plainly in Chapter 1:

"Your success is not determined by how many people you teach or help bring to baptism."

It was there the whole time. Most missionaries read right past it.

It took me a full year of frustration to understand that.

A full year believing I had failed… because I had only one baptism in twelve months.

Then, three days changed everything.

Not because anything dramatic happened, but because everything about how I saw the work shifted.

Three Days That Changed Everything

About a year into my mission, I had the opportunity to spend a few days with one of our zone leaders, Elder Mike Smith (no relation).

Those three days became a turning point, not just in my mission, but in my life.

At the time, I thought it was just a routine exchange. Years later, I learned it was intentional.

Our mission president had asked Elder Smith to spend time with me.

He had been watching me.

He saw a missionary who was unhappy… going through the motions… trying, but missing the point.

Encouragement hadn't been enough.

So he made a deliberate decision.

He sent Elder Smith not to lecture me, not to motivate me, but to create what he called *"spiritual defining experiences."*

Moments where I could feel something real.

Something undeniable.

Something that would change me.

And that's exactly what happened.

We didn't baptize anyone during those three days.

But for the first time, I understood what missionary work was really about.

What Was Different

Elder Smith approached missionary work differently than I did.

He didn't focus on numbers. He didn't stress about outcomes.

He focused on one thing:

Helping people feel the Spirit, helping them feel the Savior's love.

That was it.

No pressure.

No comparisons.

No obsession with results.

Just love.

He testified simply and sincerely, not like he was checking a box, but with his whole heart.

He used scriptures. Music. Priesthood blessings.

But more importantly, he created moments where people could *feel* something.

And after those moments, he didn't ask:

"Do you believe this?"

"Will you commit?"

He asked one simple question:

"How do you feel?"

When people responded with words like peace, warmth, comfort, or joy, he would gently testify:

"That's the Spirit."

"That's the Savior's love for you."

And you could see it happen.

Recognition.

Realization.

The moment they understood that God was speaking directly to them.

Standing on Holy Ground

During those three days, we had an experience I will never forget.

One that still stands as one of the most sacred moments of my life.

Elder Smith had been working with a family, a mother and her two children who had recently been baptized.

The father was in hospice, dying from terminal cancer.

That evening, we went to visit him.

He was weak. Barely able to speak. Barely able to move.

The room felt heavy and quiet in a way that told you something sacred was about to happen.

The family asked us to give him a priesthood blessing.

We agreed.

As we placed our hands on his head and began the blessing, tears filled the room.

The Spirit was overwhelming.

Not subtle. Not quiet.

Overwhelming.

As we finished and prepared to leave, I was the last one by his bedside.

As I turned to go, he reached out, grabbing my hand with what little strength he had left, and pulled me close.

"Kyokai ni ikitaidesu," he whispered.

"I want to go to church."

Knowing his time was short, I leaned in and quietly said:

"Mo sugu kyokai ni ikeru yo ni narimasu yo."

"You will be able to go to church soon."

I wasn't talking about this life.

He squeezed my hand.

Smiled.

And let go.

I didn't want to leave that room.

It felt like stepping off holy ground.

That moment changed me.

Not because of anything we did

but because he felt the Savior's love as he stood at heaven's door.

And so did his family.

The Shift

During those three days, I felt a kind of joy I had never experienced before.

And I made a decision.

From that point forward, I would focus on one thing:

Helping people feel the Savior's love.

Helping them recognize it.

Testifying to it.

Reminding them who they are.

That didn't mean I stopped inviting people to be baptized.

It didn't mean I became lazy or ignored goals.

It meant my focus changed.

Before:

I focused on numbers.

On performance.

On proving I was a good missionary.

After:

I focused on people.

On love.

On the Spirit.

And everything changed.

The work became joyful.

Not easy.

Not without challenges.

But filled with joy.

What I Learned About Conversion

After those three days, here's what I finally understood:

We do not convert anyone.

The Spirit does.

In the Japan Fukuoka Mission, we had a simple motto. Looking back, I now see it as a powerful framework for how the Lord does His work:

Obedience is the price.

Faith is the power.

Love is the motive.

The Spirit is the key.

Christ is the reason.

The order matters.

It's intentional.

You can't skip ahead to Christ. You can't replace the Spirit with effort, enthusiasm, or perfectly delivered lessons.

Everything in missionary work hinges on one truth:

The Spirit is the key.

You can deliver the perfect discussion. Say all the right words. Answer every question flawlessly.

But if the Spirit isn't there, nothing lasting happens.

On the other hand, you can stumble through a lesson in broken Japanese (or English, or Spanish, or whatever language you're learning). You can forget points, lose your place, and feel completely inadequate.

But when the Spirit is present, and people feel it and recognize it, that's where the miracles begin.

That's what missionary work is really about:

Helping others come unto Christ through the influence of the Spirit.

When the Spirit Softens Hearts

Let me give you a practical example from my time as a district leader in Nobeoka.

When I arrived, the relationship between the missionaries and the members was strained.

On my very first Sunday, I introduced myself to a sister in the branch.

She looked at me, said, "That's nice," and walked away.

The members weren't openly rude, but they weren't excited to see us either.

Later, I learned why.

Previous missionaries had developed a habit of showing up unannounced and staying for hours. It had worn people down.

As a district, we decided to change our approach.

If we showed up without an appointment, we didn't go inside.

We stayed in the genkan, the entryway.

We shared a brief message.

Then we asked if we could say a prayer.

In that prayer, we asked God to bless their family, their home, and to leave the Savior's love with them.

Then we left.

If we were invited back, we came by appointment, and we kept our visits to about an hour.

That was it.

Simple changes.

But the impact was profound.

I was only in Nobeoka for three months.

Yet during that time, I watched something remarkable happen.

Hearts softened.

Trust returned.

Members began inviting us back. They started helping with the work again.

Why?

Because they felt something different.

They felt respect.

They felt sincerity.

They felt the Savior's love.

And when people feel His love, things change.

That's when miracles begin.

The Scriptures Are Full of Examples

Scripture overflows with examples of the Spirit doing the converting.

Think about Alma the Younger.

His father and other church members had been praying for him for years. People had tried to teach him.

But Alma didn't change until an angel appeared, and even then, it wasn't the angel that converted him.

It was the Spirit working on his heart for three days while he lay unconscious.

When he woke, he described what happened:

"I was racked with eternal torment, for my soul was harrowed up to the greatest degree... And it came to pass that as I was thus racked with torment, while I was harrowed up by the memory of my many sins, behold, I remembered also to have heard my father prophesy... concerning... Jesus Christ... I cried: O Jesus, thou Son of God, have mercy on me... And now, behold, when I thought this, I could remember my pains no more."   *(Alma 36:12–19)*

The Spirit testified to Alma that Jesus Christ could take away his sins.

That's what converted him. Not the angel. Not his father's teachings. The Spirit.

The love of his Savior.

Think about the Lamanites in Helaman 5.

Nephi and Lehi were in prison. Fire encircled them, but they weren't burned.

A cloud of darkness covered everyone. A voice spoke peace to their souls.

And then:

"They were overshadowed with a cloud of darkness, and an awful solemn fear came upon them… And it came to pass that there came a voice… saying: Repent ye, repent ye… And behold, the Holy Spirit of God did come down from heaven, and did enter into their hearts, and they were filled as if with fire."

(Helaman 5:45)

The Holy Spirit entered their hearts. That's what converted them, not the fire Nephi and Lehi stood in.

Over and over in the scriptures, we see the same pattern:

People teach. People testify. People invite.

But the Spirit does the converting. That is why this is the most important lesson.

President Russell M. Nelson taught:

"The Holy Ghost is the minister and messenger of the Father and the Son. He testifies of both Their glorious, global reality and Their connection to us personally." ("Hear Him," General Conference, April 2020)

That's what we're helping people feel: their personal connection to God.

Elder David A. Bednar taught:

"The Holy Ghost is the third member of the Godhead... His primary roles are to testify of the Father and the Son, teach and clarify truth, warn and comfort, and sanctify the faithful." ("Receive the Holy Ghost," General Conference, October 2010)

Notice: every one of those is something the Spirit does. Not something we do.

Our job is to create an environment where the Spirit can work.

The Spirit Was Central to Christ's Ministry

Jesus Christ was the perfect teacher. He could have converted people through His words alone. Through His authority.

But He didn't. Even the Savior taught by the power of the Spirit.

Thousands watched Jesus perform miracles. They saw Him heal the sick, raise the dead, walk on water, and feed five thousand people with a few loaves and fish.

And yet many of those same people later turned away from Him.

Some who witnessed His greatest miracles stood in the crowd shouting, "Crucify Him!" just days later.

The miracles didn't convert them. The miracles didn't bring lasting change.

You know what brought lasting change? The Spirit.

Look at the people who stayed. The ones who became His true disciples.

Peter, James, and John didn't follow Jesus because of miracles. They followed Him because the Spirit testified to their hearts that He was the Son of God.

When Jesus asked Peter,

"Whom say ye that I am?" Peter responded: "Thou art the Christ, the Son of the living God."

And Jesus said to him,

"Blessed art thou, Simon Bar-jona: for flesh and blood hath not revealed it unto thee, but my Father which is in heaven."

Matthew 16:15–17

The Father revealed it through the Spirit. Not through miracles. Not through impressive teaching. Through the Spirit bearing witness to Peter's heart.

That's the kind of conversion that lasts. That's the kind of conversion you're helping people find.

In 3 Nephi, after His resurrection, Jesus appears to the Nephites.

He teaches them. Blesses their children. Gives them the sacrament.

"They did not multiply many words, for it was given unto them what they should pray, and they were filled with desire… And when he had said these words, he himself also knelt upon the earth; and behold, he prayed unto the Father… and the things which he prayed cannot be written." (3 Nephi 19:24–32)

Even Jesus prayed to the Father. Even He relied on the Spirit to teach.

If the Savior of the world taught by the Spirit, how much more should we?

He also taught His disciples:

"It is not ye that speak, but the Spirit of your Father which speaketh in you."

(Matthew 10:20)

Your job isn't to have all the answers. It's to be a conduit for the Spirit.

I didn't understand any of this while I was grinding through my first year, frustrated and convinced I was failing. It took those three days with Elder Smith to show me that the Savior's example wasn't just scripture to study, it was the way to actually do this work. Once I started following it, the work became joyful.

Practical Applications

So what does this look like day to day?

Before you knock on a door. Before you teach a lesson. Before you start a conversation, pray.

But not a quick, routine prayer.

This is a sincere plea:

"Father, I can't do this without Thee. Please help them feel Thy love through me."

Then create moments where people can feel something.

Use scriptures to help them recognize God's love for them.

Use inspiring, sacred music to stir their hearts.

Share your testimony of a loving Heavenly Father and your Savior. Share the personal experiences that helped you gain that testimony.

But don't rush.

Give people time to sit with what they're feeling.

Silence is okay. It's not awkward.

It's sacred.

Then ask them how they feel.

This is the key.

Don't ask, "Do you feel the Spirit?"

Ask, "How do you feel right now?"

Or, "What's one word that describes what you're feeling?"

Let them describe it in their own words.

When they say things like peace, warmth, comfort, or joy, testify with sincerity:

"That feeling you just described, that's the Spirit of the Lord. That's God speaking to your heart. That's the Savior's love for you."

Help them connect the feeling to its source.

If someone says they don't feel anything, don't panic.

Invite them to act.

"Would you be willing to pray tonight and ask God if what we taught today is true?"

"Would you read this chapter and pay attention to how you feel?"

Action opens the door for the Spirit to work.

At the end of each day, ask yourself:

Did I help people feel the Savior's love today?

Did I create moments for the Spirit to work?

Did I testify with sincerity?

If the answer is yes, you had a successful day regardless of whether anyone committed to baptism.

As taught:

"You can know that the Lord is pleased with your efforts as you feel the Spirit working through you." *(Church Handbook of Instruction, 4.2.8)*

A Final Thought

Again, I'm not saying baptisms don't matter.

They do. Baptism is an essential ordinance, the gateway to everything else.

But it shouldn't be your focus.

If you focus on helping people feel and recognize the Spirit, you are successful.

Some people will be baptized while you're there.

Some won't be baptized until years later.

Some may never be baptized in this life.

But if you help them feel the Savior's love, you've done your job.

After those three days with Elder Smith, everything changed.

I stopped stressing about baptism numbers.

I stopped comparing myself to other missionaries.

I stopped measuring my worth by statistics.

I simply focused on helping people feel His love.

And when I did… I found joy.

Not the fleeting happiness that comes from hitting a goal, but deep, lasting joy that comes from being an instrument in God's hands.

The kind of joy that made it almost unbearable to leave when my mission ended.

The Spirit is the most important ally you have as a missionary.

More important than your language skills.

More important than your knowledge of the scriptures.

More important than your ability to answer every question.

Your role is simple:

Be a conduit.

Be a vessel.

Be an instrument.

Invite the Spirit.

Create moments where people can feel.

Ask how they feel and testify to what they're experiencing.

Do that, and you will have a successful mission.

And when it's time to go home, it will break your heart to leave the people you've come to love.

A Promise

I promise you this:

If you focus on helping people feel and recognize the Spirit, you will love being a missionary.

You will be filled with joy as you watch hearts soften and open to the Savior's love.

That dying man in the hospice facility in Japan didn't need me to baptize him.

He needed to feel the Savior's love in his final days.

And when he did, when the Spirit testified to his heart that Jesus Christ is real, and that he would see Him again, that was the power of the Spirit working in his life.

For You to Ponder and Act

- Think of one person you served or taught, someone you felt you "failed" because there was no visible outcome. Now reconsider that experience using only these four questions: Did I work hard?

  Did I love them?

  Did I teach truth?

  Did I follow the Spirit as best I could?

- Tonight, and every night this week, measure your day using only those same four questions. Nothing else.

For Parents and Leaders

- When someone you love returns from a mission, what do you ask about first? What would change if you started with their heart instead of their results?

- Think of one missionary, youth, or ward member whose effort and compassion you have never specifically acknowledged. Find a way to do that this week.

Before You Leave

You don't convert people on a mission.

You help them feel the Savior's love and recognize what they're feeling.

That's it.

And you can start practicing now.

In a Sunday School class.

In a conversation with a struggling friend.

In a fast and testimony meeting.

Learn to create space for the Spirit.

Learn to testify from your own experience, not from a script.

The missionaries who understand this before they leave are the ones who hit the ground running.

Start now, and you'll be ahead of where I was for the entire first year of my mission.

KEEP WALKING

I would never say that my two years in Japan were the best years of my life.

Life has given me far greater gifts since then: marriage, fatherhood, and now the blessing of being a grandfather. These are among the greatest callings I have ever known.

But I will say this without hesitation:

Those two years were the best two years for my life.

That is where my ongoing conversion began.

That is where I came to know my Savior not as a concept, not as a doctrine, but as my Redeemer and my friend.

I often think about how close I came to missing that conversion.

Three days with Elder Mike Smith changed the entire trajectory of my mission and my life.

Before those days, I was grinding through missionary work, measuring success by numbers instead of hearts.

After those days, I was different.

I stopped trying to manage outcomes and started trying to help people feel the Savior's love.

I am eternally grateful for Elder Smith, for President and Sister Figuerres, and for every companion, missionary, and member who loved me when I didn't think I deserved it.

They showed me what Christlike service looks like.

They were and continue to be instruments in my conversion.

Most of all, I am grateful for a Savior who never gave up on me.

I failed often on my mission.

I got discouraged.

I lost focus.

I made mistakes.

That is normal, not just for missionaries, but for life.

Yet He never stopped teaching me, refining me, or loving me.

He simply invited me, again and again, to begin anew.

President Figuerres taught me that missionaries who serve with a gospel-centered heart, motivated by love for God and for the people He places in their path, become permanently different.

The ministering does not stop when they go home.

The love does not stop when a calling ends.

It becomes part of who they are.

Missionaries who focus only on the organization, the numbers, and the tasks often return home unchanged.

The gospel gave them a job, but never transformed their hearts.

Don't let that be your story.

After more than thirty years of reflection, here is what I know:

You are sent where you are sent for a reason.

Every area.

Every companion.

Every challenge.

Trust the Lord, even when you cannot see His plan.

When the work feels heavy, ask Him one simple question:

"Do You love me?"

He will answer.

He always does in His time and in His way.

Baptisms are the byproduct of genuine conversion to Jesus Christ.

The Spirit is the key to every spiritual process: conversion, repentance, growth, and change.

Help people feel the Savior's love and recognize His voice, and you will begin to understand what missionary work is truly about.

The Spirit speaks differently to each of us.

Some feel warmth.

Some feel peace.

Some receive words.

Some simply know.

What matters is not how He speaks, but that you learn to recognize His voice and trust it.

You may never know in this life whose heart you touched or when the seeds you planted will finally grow.

That was never your responsibility.

Faithfulness is.

You are a spirit son or daughter of God.

You are His disciple.

You are doing His work.

And He knows you by name.

In Gethsemane, Jesus Christ experienced every moment of your life, every doubt, every failure, every lonely night on your knees in a foreign country, wondering if anyone loves you.

He knows exactly how you feel because He felt it too.

That is not doctrine at a distance.

That is a Savior close enough to catch you when you begin to sink.

I know He lives.

I know He is my Redeemer.

And I know He is my friend.

My prayer is that through your mission, through every door you knock, every seed you plant, and every person you love in His name, He will become your friend too.

Keep walking with Him.

CHAPTER QUICK-REFERENCE GUIDE

Learning to Walk with Him: Five Lessons from the Mission Field

---

For parents, youth leaders, and missionaries who want to know what's inside each chapter.

CHAPTER ONE

You Never Know Who You Will Touch

And if it so be that you should labor all your days in crying repentance unto this people, and bring, save it be one soul unto me, how great shall be your joy with him in the kingdom of my Father!

Doctrine and Covenants 18:15

> **JAPANESE KOTOWAZA** 一期一会 (Ichi-go ichi-e) "One time, one meeting."
> Every encounter is unique and will never recur in the same way, treasure each moment and person.

CORE LESSON: Every person a missionary meets matters, even when the impact remains unseen.

WHAT THIS CHAPTER IS ABOUT

A story of returning to Japan three years after completing a mission and meeting a woman nearly forgotten. One door contact. One afternoon playing with her children in the hallway while a companion spoke with her. One transfer, and she vanished from memory. Three years later, in a chapel in Nobeoka, she walked up and said she had just been baptized.

From that experience comes a foundational truth: many seeds sprout long after a missionary has gone home. That doesn't mean the work was wasted. It means the Lord is still working.

STORIES INSIDE THIS CHAPTER

- A woman in Japan baptized three years after one brief door contact

- The parable of the seed from Alma 32 and what it teaches missionaries

- Paul and Apollos: one planted, one watered, God gave the increase

- Ammon using the word "perhaps" after years of sacrifice and prison

WHAT A YOUTH, PARENT, OR LEADER WILL FIND HERE

- A reality check on baptism numbers as the measure of missionary success

- Comfort for missionaries who feel they are accomplishing nothing

- Encouragement to love everyone, even those who say no, because they may say yes years later

- A framework for understanding the role of planter, waterer, or harvester

- Permission to trust God with the harvest rather than carry that weight alone

QUESTION TO ASK YOUR MISSIONARY:

"Who did you meet this week that you might never see again? What small kindness did you show them?"

CHAPTER TWO

You Are Sent Where You Are Sent for a Reason

Trust in the Lord with all thine heart; and lean not unto thine own understanding. In all thy ways acknowledge him, and he shall direct thy paths.

Proverbs 3:5–6

> **JAPANESE KOTOWAZA** 適材適所 (Tekizai tekisho) "The right person in the right place."
>
> Everything and everyone has a purpose in the place they are assigned.

CORE LESSON: Mission calls and area transfers are inspired. The purpose is often invisible until later, but it is never accidental.

WHAT THIS CHAPTER IS ABOUT

A mission call to Japan, received with zero enthusiasm. No interest in Asian culture. Hated seafood. Went anyway. Years later, every single area revealed a specific purpose completely missed in the moment.

The chapter also follows a young woman from the ward who received a stateside mission call and felt discouraged by it. She went anyway. After returning home, she wept when asked whether mission calls are inspired. She now knew the answer for herself.

STORIES INSIDE THIS CHAPTER

- Opening that Japan mission call and sitting in silence, not happy about it

- A teenage girl in Kita Kyushu baptized after a prompting to invite her, then an immediate transfer

- A difficult companion who taught a hard lesson: pride dressed up as patience is still pride

- President and Sister Figuerres, who loved and mentored without judgment, and still do thirty years later

- Jonah and Esther as scriptural parallels for being sent somewhere that makes no sense

WHAT A YOUTH, PARENT, OR LEADER WILL FIND HERE

- A direct, honest answer to the question: Are mission calls actually inspired?

- Help for missionaries disappointed by their call, or a transfer they didn't want

- A reframe for "why am I here" thinking: do the work now; the reason will come later

- The Savior's own example of being sent where the Father needed Him, not where it was comfortable

- An honest look at difficult companions and what those situations are sometimes really for

> "You were never in the wrong place. Not even once. The Lord knew exactly what He was doing, even when you had no clue."

QUESTION TO ASK YOUR MISSIONARY:

"Is there anything about where you are right now that is starting to make more sense?"

CHAPTER THREE

Keep the Savior's Life and Ministry as Your Focus

But seek ye first the kingdom of God, and his righteousness; and all these things shall be added unto you.

Matthew 6:33

> **JAPANESE KOTOWAZA** 初心忘るべからず (Shoshin wasuru bekarazu) "Never forget your original intention."
>
> Even as you gain experience, don't lose sight of why you started in the first place.

CORE LESSON: When focus shifts off Christ, everything falls apart. When eyes stay on Him, even the hardest days become bearable.

WHAT THIS CHAPTER IS ABOUT

Near the end of a mission, serving as a zone leader, an alarm goes off and a bed feels impossible to leave. A song lyric enters the mind: Not one regret, true to the end. The Savior knew what was coming and pressed forward anyway. That single thought got a missionary out of bed.

The chapter also tells the story of a son returning home early from his mission, and a father's failure in that moment to ask what the Savior would do. A father-in-law asks one quiet question that

135

changes everything: "Your son needs his bishop." It is the most honest chapter in the book.

STORIES INSIDE THIS CHAPTER

- The morning the alarm went off and getting up felt impossible, and the song lyric that changed it

- Peter walking on water: what happens the moment you take your eyes off Christ

- A son returning home early from his mission, and a father sitting in the living room seething at God

- A father-in-law's quiet correction: "Your son needs his bishop"

- Jesus at the well with a Samaritan woman and at the tree with Zacchaeus: ministry one person at a time

- The mission goal math that humbled a zone leader who thought the numbers weren't working

WHAT A YOUTH, PARENT, OR LEADER WILL FIND HERE

- A real answer for missionaries grinding through the work without any joy

- The most vulnerable chapter in the book, including admitting anger at God and pride in suffering

- A practical reset question, "What would Jesus do?", applied to specific missionary frustrations

- How to measure a day by love and ministry rather than statistics

- A reminder that the Atonement of Jesus Christ is not just for forgiveness, it is the power to keep going

> "Never let a problem to be solved become more important than a person to be loved." President Thomas S. Monson

QUESTION TO ASK YOUR MISSIONARY:

"When things got hard this week, what did you do to refocus on the Savior?"

CHAPTER FOUR

Don't Underestimate the Power of Prayer

But thou, when thou prayest, enter into thy closet, and when thou hast shut thy door, pray to thy Father which is in secret; and thy Father which seeth in secret shall reward thee openly.

Matthew 6:6

JAPANESE KOTOWAZA 石の上にも三年 (Ishi no ue ni mo san nen) "Three years on a cold stone."

With patience and persistence, even sitting on a cold stone for three years will warm it.

Keep praying, keep trusting, even when nothing seems to be happening.

CORE LESSON: The Lord hears. The Lord answers. And sometimes five simple words are enough to carry a missionary through anything.

WHAT THIS CHAPTER IS ABOUT

Early in the mission, alone in a bedroom in Japan, completely overwhelmed and questioning everything, one prayer is offered: "Do You love me?" What happens next becomes the spiritual anchor of the entire mission. Arms felt around the shoulders. Five words, clear as day: "Elder Smith, I love you."

That same prayer returns later, during the long stretch of leading a zone alone, no companion, drowning in responsibility. The answer comes again. Knowing the Lord's love is enough to carry on. The chapter builds outward from there into a teaching on sincere prayer and the army of people praying for missionaries in temples around the world every single week.

STORIES INSIDE THIS CHAPTER

- A bedroom in Japan, a closed door, and five words that became a mission's anchor

- Leading a zone alone for weeks, overwhelmed, and returning to that same simple prayer

- Enos wrestling before God in the woods, and what real prayer actually looks like

- The Brother of Jared: prayer requires effort, creativity, and showing up with your best solution

- Every endowment session in every temple on earth almost always includes a prayer for the missionaries

WHAT A YOUTH, PARENT, OR LEADER WILL FIND HERE

- A word-for-word account of what sincere missionary prayer can feel like

- Comfort for missionaries who feel alone, forgotten, or spiritually dry

- The difference between routine prayer and real, vulnerable conversation with God

- Practical application: pray for companions by name, keep a prayer journal, ask the simple question

- A reminder that discouragement is a tool of the adversary, and prayer is the counter

> "Do You love me?" Ask that question sincerely. The Lord will answer. And that answer will give you the strength to keep going.

QUESTION TO ASK YOUR MISSIONARY:

"Have you felt the Lord's love for you lately? If not, have you asked Him directly?"

CHAPTER FIVE

Baptisms Are Not the Focus, the Savior's Love Is

But the Comforter, which is the Holy Ghost, whom the Father will send in my name, he shall teach you all things, and bring all things to your remembrance, whatsoever I have said unto you.

John 14:26

> **JAPANESE KOTOWAZA** 心に響く (Kokoro ni hibiku) "To resound in the heart."
>
> When truth strikes the heart, it creates a resonance that cannot be denied. This is how the Spirit works.

CORE LESSON: Missionaries do not convert anyone. The Spirit does. When the focus shifts from numbers to helping people feel the Savior's love, everything about the mission changes.

WHAT THIS CHAPTER IS ABOUT

One year into the mission, frustrated, comparing, running on fumes, I spend three days with a zone leader named Elder Smith. No baptisms come from those three days. They are still the best three days of my entire mission, because all we do is help people feel the Spirit and then help them recognize what they felt.

The chapter's most sacred moment unfolds in a hospice facility, where we give a priesthood blessing to a dying man. Afterward, he reaches out and grabs a missionary's hand: "I want to go to church." The whispered answer: "You will be able to soon." Both of us knew we were not talking about this life.

STORIES INSIDE THIS CHAPTER

- Three days with Elder Smith and the complete shift in how missionary work is understood

- A hospice visit: a dying man, a priesthood blessing, and five words that brought comfort

- The method Elder Smith taught: "How do you feel?" followed by testifying of the Spirit's source

- Changing the culture in Nobeoka: how one district repaired a damaged relationship with members

- Alma the Younger and the Lamanites in Helaman 5: the Spirit does the converting, not the missionary

WHAT A YOUTH, PARENT, OR LEADER WILL FIND HERE

- The most important chapter in the book

- A specific, repeatable method for helping people feel and recognize the Spirit

- Relief for missionaries burning out from chasing baptism goals

- A way to measure mission success that produces joy instead of anxiety

- Why missions focused on the Spirit often produce more baptisms, not fewer

> "The Spirit is the most important ally you can have as a missionary. More important than your language skills. More important than your knowledge of the scriptures. The Spirit is who does the converting. Not you."

QUESTION TO ASK YOUR MISSIONARY:

"Did anyone feel the Spirit this week? What happened when they did?"

ABOUT THE AUTHOR

Ken Smith served as a missionary in the Japan Fukuoka Mission from 1991 to 1993 under Mission President Cyril I. A. Figuerres, an experience that shaped his testimony and his understanding of what it means to truly walk with the Savior.

After returning home, Ken has spent nearly two decades investing in the faith lives of young people. He served as a bishop in The Church of Jesus Christ of Latter-day Saints, and later as a counselor in his stake presidency with responsibility for youth programs. During his years as bishop, he personally addressed a letter to the young men and women in his ward who received a mission call, the letter that eventually became this book.

At the time of publication, Ken serves on a Young Single Adult stake high council alongside his wife, continuing the work of preparing and supporting the rising generation of missionaries and disciples.

Ken's most cherished roles are husband, father, and grandfather. He holds a senior leadership role in technology and lives in the Pacific Northwest. He remains close to President and Sister Figuerres, the mission president and companion who shaped his service in Japan, who continue to mentor and influence his life more than thirty years later.

Learning to Walk with Him is his first book.